What I Missed: 12 Lessons on Life and Business

By Bill Quinn

Website: www.equinnconsulting.com

ISBN-13: 978-1541032996

ISBN-10: 1541032993

Dedication

I want to dedicate this book to my mom who didn't have the opportunity to provide the valued things like self-esteem and self-actualization to her children. I admired what she could do however for providing for us to the best of her abilities. This is my thank you mom for instilling a healthy work ethic in me and my siblings.

To my wife, Barb, son Pierre, daughter Ashleigh, daughter-in-law Coleen, granddaughters Briana and Ella. You all are a blessing to me and thank you for your inspiration and support. I am blessed to have such a family. I could have never imagined such a wonderful family as a young person growing up. God has surely blessed me with your presence in my life.

Introduction

Having spent all my fifty-eight years of life searching for my identity, entering a life of business was a natural extension of my early years on the farm. "What I Missed: In Life and Business" is a short version of my life experiences and the many missing components that caused shortcoming because of my own lack of understanding and that of the experience by those that raised me as a child. As I have worked on creating this discussion, I wanted to say something that would resonate with whomever would read this first writing. After getting the first draft through the first edit I became quite clear of the need for the message that I originally wrote to heal the void in my soul, but I now know so many others have the same void.

I visited a close aunt who had knee surgery this past summer, just to show her respect and I cared about our family relationship. When I learned from our short visit was her having exactly my experience in missing of a relationship with her father that left a void in her soul.

Last year on a two-hour trip to New Orleans International airport I had a conversation with one of my brothers-in-law about an almost identical experience in his life that mirrored my experience.

I did research for an experiential class narrative and found extensive information on large percentages of children coming into life missing key relationships and conditions that leave them confuse and disconnected.

The purpose of this book revolves around my business experience and what I missed in those experiences. What I have learned from this experience is accepting the things that I missed and messed up has great healing factors and reminding me not to make those mistakes again.

There are millions who have missed out on opportunities, jobs, business ventures, family relationships, marriages, finishing high school or college, and what I want to share is don't let those missed experiences keep you in the past or believing you can't continue to the next summit or horizon in your life.

One of the What I Missed in my life has had a profound impact on all my life experiences, is finding my identity, this life experience reverberated through my years, causing me to miss other experiences and relationships. I went to my family reunion for the first time after 44 years, realizing how much I missed in positive relationships and realizing the connectedness and similarity of character of so many of my cousins, was refreshing. My achiever personality fit right in with many in my generation and those in generations before and after me. It was most astonishing to experience, and sad that I had missed these vital connections, in my quest to find myself through my missing father. My challenge to my audience, if you are on the road I traveled seeking a missing parent, find a solid relationship with someone that can help you grow and develop. And for those that see a child that has a missing parent do what you can to instill positive influences to guide that young person who lacks a positive parental experience, when the opportunity presents itself.

My experience of missing parental relations shaped my school life, nuclear family life, and my business life. How you are raised has a direct impact on how you will raise your children, conduct yourself in school, function on the job or manage your business.

What I want you to get from my experiences if you are in the same kind of experience, is make a positive change, if you see someone having this kind of experience, give them hope and inspiration, and if you have lived this kind of experience as I have, do your very best to end it in your posterity. The relationship that my son and daughter have with me and their mom is a complete contrast to the life my wife and I had with our parents. This was done with complete intent.

No matter how your life started, you are in control of how it ends, you can choose how the story will be written for the balance of your life.

Willie (Bill) Quinn

When you finally go back to your old hometown, you find it wasn't the old home you missed but your childhood.

Sam Ewing, former baseball player.

Table of Contents

What I Missed: Fears

My early years were filled with fears that were mostly unjustified. I think that the greatest fear I had was not finding my identity. I spent most of my time trying to figure out why I was so afraid of failing, living up to someone else's standards, wanting to be loved, and wishing that my family would show me affections that they cared for me. I never remember anyone telling me not to be afraid as a child growing up, so I never really had the confidence not to be afraid. That greatest fear of failing stayed with me for most of my life, up until the last five years or so. When I left my job with a secure paycheck, my fears of failure started to subside. While in the family business, I was consumed with the thought of failure that manifested itself. As I'll mention in other chapters, when I left the motivation, confidence building, and character development environment, I was experiencing in my first love of the real estate industry. I was afraid of the constant vicissitudes of the real estate business cycle, and the letdowns of a culture that did not support a truly talented and sincere professional because of skin pigmentation. So when we achieved the success of getting my mom into the first operation, fear and lack of understanding continued to drive me. Having qualified enough homebuyers and sellers, I knew enough to understand that I had the talent to gain greater income, which was one of the keys to unlocking the doors to success. Actually, helping my mom go into business was also my seeking income to fill in the cycles associated with real estate sales.

What I didn't realize was that fear of failure drew failure to me; meaning that the thing I dreaded the most was eventually going to occur because I focused on the fear of failing and not the opportunities for success that were always at my fingertips. What I forgot were things like Earl Nightingale's "acres of diamonds," and that my limitations had spurred my imagination to the heights we had already achieved. I was stuck, not realizing that I needed to return to an environment that had invigorated the success we had.

I was relentless in staying in an environment that I understand today was toxic and which knew nothing of individual development. After opening the second dry-cleaning operation, so many opportunities became available to me, but I lacked the wisdom to listen to the person that had my best interest at heart and wanted us to move away to start a life for ourselves. I was offered a position to go to Adrian, Michigan, a college town about twenty minutes from the Ohio border, for an appraisal company that I had worked for about eight months and I guess I impressed them enough to offer me a position to relocate to their main office.

The reason I didn't take the offer, which was life-changing for someone with my attitude and aptitude, was because I felt my mom and brother could not manage the businesses without me. The real reason was fear—of the unknown, never having anyone in my life that supported and advocated personal growth and change. I was afraid that I would not live up to the challenge even though I had already proven myself by performing in the position. I was scared because there was no one in the town that I had seen when I visited who looked like me. So, I stayed put, rationalizing that my mom and brother needed me to manage the businesses.

Having many similar experiences; another time while still in the family business I allowed the fear of success to take over. While selling real estate, I had impressed a new medical director from General Motors who had decided to make her home purchase from me. I backed out of helping her because I would not face the challenge of helping her find a new home in higher-end locations while wrestling with a new business opening. This would have been another breakthrough for my real estate career, but I opted to stay within the comfortable confines of the family business.

Though the successes within our family business were monumental based on the context of where we started from and the many milestones we achieved, I foolishly missed staying connected to the dreams and aspirations that provided the education and experiences that led to establishing the family businesses in the first place.

My wife and I have many discussions about our environment and how staying within a limiting group of people limited our successes. Having a family and culture that advocates mediocrity and denounces excelling contributed partly to our not moving away, and finding an environment and community that promoted growth and achievements.

This can be difficult coming from an experience where many communities of affluence would not allow someone of color to enter.

After spending the last four years in my own business, my fears have started to melt away, not so much because I have made the achievements I sought, but because I have learned that fear and worry accomplished only one thing—wasted time. Again, listening to Earl Nightingale: "If you can't change it, if it's in the past, why waste time with it in your thoughts." Another thing that Nightingale reminded me was to keep a watchful eye on your confidence by feeding it with positive self-affirmations. Make this an everyday practice. Feeding your mind with positive self-confidence messages and experiences removes the negative junk of many years of close negative associations.

What I Missed: The Takeaways

The chance to experience other communities and people who did the things that my wife and I enjoyed, like reading, writing, getting our children a better education, and living a peaceful and drama less life, while excelling in our profession. Spending time with people that aspired for personal development, and lived with a purpose.

1. An aspiring business owner should pick his/her environment carefully, even if it means finding somewhere outside of your current family and community.

2. If you have fears, get help with dealing with whatever the root of your fears. Fill your days creating and completing small accomplishments that when you look back on them, you will see rows of success. Each task completed builds your confidence.

3. Read and listen to positive books and motivating journals and publications, with God's message at the center.

4. Most importantly, shut off your **television**. It is a positive thought killer and replace it with independent thinking.

5. Associate with people that have something constructive to offer you, and are willing and appreciate what you offer. Negative people will keep fear alive, so stay away from these type of personalities and environments.

6. The interesting thing that happens today is that I am drawn to all types of personalities, but I have learned to stay away or leave individuals and groups that only have their own best interest in mind. If I find that I have become exposed to individuals and/or groups that have manipulative negative thinking and actions, I quickly move on. I would recommend strongly that you do likewise. For your business to be successful, you will need all the positive support, energy, and activities you can muster.

"Whenever we're afraid, it's because we don't know enough. If we understood enough, we would never be afraid."
Earl Nightingale, Dean of Personal Development

What I Missed: Roles and Responsibilities

This chapter is the most intriguing for me because of the importance of clearly defined roles and responsibilities. Let me start out by saying that this can make or break your organization. When we started, my primary objective was to replace my mom's income from her previous long-term employer. After having very good success with the first business, I recognized the need for greater income to support more than one household. What didn't take place is a discussion where we decided on roles and responsibilities. I had my ideas of how the business should be developed, and my mom was excited to have her own shop and a source of income. I don't believe she thought about the future the same way I did. What I later realized was that I had helped her achieve her dream and she had no aspirations for anything higher. The role I stepped into was the same as what I did to get the businesses started; I was performing functions like reviewing and developing contractual agreements, doing my best to get everyone's understanding, addressing legal and administrative issues as they arose. What I didn't stop to consider was that since my mom was the owner of the business, and eventually businesses, she should have been at the forefront of these activities.

So, I took on the role of getting these things done, first because they were needed, and secondly because my mom was not able to perform them. I maintained a mother-son relationship when it had shifted to a business-partner relationship, and the same thing manifested for my younger brother. We continued in this fashion for most of the business's existence. My primary reasoning was a belief that I held from my real estate career, which was to never do any harm to a buyer or seller. Knowing that I could talk someone into something and it could be a financial disaster, I always wanted the best outcome for anyone I did business with. I never got the nerve nor had the experience to address this vital aspect of business functions.

A further countermeasure was a view by another sibling that I was taking advantage of my mom. What was wrong with that perspective was—and I mean no disrespect toward my mom—she lacked the skills to take the businesses to the next level, and I think that the action taken was the best way to stay in control. I never wanted to be viewed as someone who would take advantage of anyone, especially my mom. I never wanted to take control nor demand what was rightfully my brother's and mine. Because of these unclear roles and responsibilities, my younger brother and I were the ones taken advantage of. Our primary goal was to make a living for our mom and ourselves; however, we were never given ownership in a proper manner, because our contributions were as significant as hers.

One fundamental that I aspired for was recognizing my mom and sibling's skills in our varied work life experiences. I felt that if we could do the same in our own business, we could build a great organization. All of us were great employees for other businesses and organizations, and if this could be harnessed for ourselves, our accomplishments could be unlimited.

Our family business experience was largely an experience in family bonding dynamics or lack thereof. The day I wrote this chapter, I read an article that crystallized my family's experience, and I'm sure this will resonate with many people involved in small or large independent businesses. This person had gone into business with a family member, and found that it was a bad move to make because he was jaded in terms of what he was seeing in the other person. What he looked at was all the wrong things; they brought money and some skills, but they had no real knowledge about managing a process or people. He was trusting where he should be analyzing, thinking that his partner knew how to handle certain affairs, but later found out that he didn't. He wasn't checking because they had always been close, but never asked if the senior partner knew how to handle certain tasks, and found out later that the partner was not as great of an asset as he'd first perceived.

Because of our lack of clarity in roles and responsibilities, we made no real, defined plans. I felt that the business needed to grow and thrive. In contrast, my mom was very comfortable in a small shop mentality, and I didn't realize this until she asked me one day after we had made multiple expansions and developments, why I thought so big. It hit me then how incompatible we were. By this time, we were in our fifth operation and because I was highly instrumental in all the developments, I knew then that I had been on the wrong path.

I expected this harmonious attitude from my family. I attempted to communicate, but didn't have any skills at getting messages across, particularly this most profound vision. My biggest weakness was that I could think of great ideas, but I lacked the ability to convey the message, at least to my siblings (or was I speaking to the wrong crowd?). I expected my mom to respect what I did for her and the businesses, but never made it clear what I wanted out of the business, expecting her to do the right thing. Part of me today realizes that I had taken my mom and my family members so far outside of their environment and experiences, that it probably seemed like I was probably out of my mind to most of them.

We knew the technical aspects of our businesses very well, but like many small business owners, we lacked the administrative side of business and the exposure to other successful operations, even in other industries. We had no experience in things like how to build a team, how to gain additional business and management skills, or how to seek the latest industry trends and benchmarks. These were not at the forefront of our activities. We could build operational and technical teams but lacked the ability, skills, and opportunity to build our administrative team by bringing in talent from the outside to help us grow. I think that if we were bonded as siblings, we would have had greater success. Bonding would have resulted in a trust among ourselves, which would have given us the ability to select the right outside talent.

We knew our workflow and processes like the back of our hand, but we never committed them to a formal document so that they could be shared with other team members.

What I Missed: Takeaway

The takeaway I want to leave you with is to know who you are going into business with, especially family members. Don't be afraid to ask the hard questions. Look for compatible traits and make sure the partnership is equitable. It should not matter if the leader is the younger person; this is something that often flies in the face of certain ethnicities.

1. What you want are business partners that have similar goals, aspirations, and a mindset to learn and grow. Find a template, if you are not able to create your own, of an organization chart or list of business roles and responsibilities. Write them out and list who will be doing what. Be honest. If you can't do the job, let your partners take the role or hire from outside.

2. All members of the business should be willing and assertive about learning, from as many settings as your business will allow: business classes, onsite or off-site seminars or webinars, etc. You can bring experts in your industry to present the latest techniques, methods, and trends to your team, or visit the facilities of noncompetitive industry leaders to give insight to your team on the possibilities of your business success.

3. If you are in a business relationship that is on the ropes, get professional help. Family Magazine is a publication I subscribe to, as an example. There are many great family business teams out there. If you are struggling in yours, seek someone who may be willing to share how they accomplished maintaining a great relationship. Don't be afraid to stop and negotiate a buyout, settlement, or possibly closing. There is nothing wrong with changing directions when you realize that you are going down the wrong path.

4. Other high-level perspectives you want in your business, if you are just getting started or struggling with internal conflicts, or searching for a way to promote a team relationship concept. If you have infighting, consider a truce and get some help from outside professionals. We often will listen to someone else when we are in conflict in close relationships, so find a skilled mediator.

5. Whatever is going on within the core of the business with leaders will manifest itself in the employees and will eventually be observed and felt by your customers, so make every possible effort to create strong bonds within your core group.

If the core of your business is positive or negative, it will show up in your community and customers. For family businesses and small businesses in general, make it a profound part of your process to get your roles and responsibilities clear with everyone in your operations. Family businesses can oftentimes let things fester without any real intent to make changes, dragging yourself and your business down. Get into a space where you are truthful, straightforward, and humbly blunt about the weaknesses and threats that you, your partners, and your employees have. An evaluation of the strengths and weaknesses of your team members should be a high priority. Many days are hectic with staying on top of servicing customers, but planning sessions into your work week that address your internal relationships will make customer relations easier to maintain. I know that you have heard this said before, but without great bonds on roles and responsibilities with your internal partners and employees, you can't deliver to your key partners, your customers!!!

And one standing alone can be attacked and defeated, but two can stand back-to-back and conquer; three is even better, for a triple-braided cord is not easily broken.

Ecclesiastes 4:12 TLB.

What I Missed: Business Structure I

Initially, we acquired Downtown Valet Cleaners and filed an Assumed Name affidavit with the county clerk's office, and we had a legal business entity. We didn't realize or have the knowledge at the time that we were very exposed from a liability perspective; all our business and personal resources were at risk. We functioned as a sole proprietor for about nine years. During that time, I suggested that we incorporate the business, not realizing that I didn't have the respect of my mom and younger brother and it prevented them from agreeing to have the business structure changed to a corporation.

A further missed opportunity was the lack of a legal counselor with a strong business background to guide us in our business affairs. I knew we needed professional advisors on our team; the difficulty was finding them. Many of the legal professionals in our community operated in a capricious manner, meaning they had no interest in helping someone develop. The only interest they appeared to have was if you had money or if they could get a big case from you.

Having known the difference between a general practitioner and a specialist or someone who practices criminal law and someone who practices business, real estate, estate planning, or corporate law. In structuring our initial purchase, we used a real estate attorney to review our documents and help us with closing the sale, but I did not consider him when we got into a legal case with our second operation. I made the mistake of using a local general practitioner and wanting to do business with someone from our community. In hindsight, that was one of the biggest mistakes I made. We were not afforded the respect of a professional from our community, yet we had earned respect from someone outside the community, I let my wanting to be supportive in our community put our business plans at risk.

During that same process, we had another need for a business legal advisor. We had decided to set up our second operation as a dry store, meaning we would not do dry cleaning onsite, saving the cost of chemicals and workforce at this location. We checked with the state and received guidelines on how to complete the process, and thus, we did not need a state license to operate.

The city where we were located had not dealt with the type of business we had arranged, so there was no precedence on their books that would allow them to issue a city license to a dry-cleaning store that did not need a state license or a dry store. It took us weekly city council meetings in which we tried to get the council to see that we had state clearance to operate and that they did not license our type of operation. After many months, I finally got the council and a representative from the licensing division to understand what the state regulatory agency had arranged and that this was common in other communities. We eventually got the city license. The moral of the story is, we won the battle, but lost the war. Having concentrated our efforts on saving the business, we had to close our second operation immediately after getting the licensure issue resolved, due to using up resources from our first operation to maintain the second operation and not being able to complete our plans for the second store, along with a failed legal dispute. We needed legal counsel in this matter that could have helped navigate governmental red tape and bureaucratic processes; having such an expert could have expedited this process. It would have cost us considerable legal fees, but it also would have left us with what we didn't have after twenty-two months, which was time, energy, and financing to continue.

Our biggest mistake was having all our businesses as sole proprietorships and later in one corporation. It was not the best of moves. When we were forced to close, we had to close everything.

We eventually incorporated as a Subchapter S entity on December 22, 1993, after making many significant business transactions including being awarded one of our largest contracts.

What we didn't have was the knowledge to place our businesses into separate corporate entities which could potentially have protected us. If one failed, we could have maintained the others.

What I Missed - Takeaways

1. Use every resource you can to find a qualified attorney and place them on a retainer. We often looked at having someone on retainer as a burden, not as an advantage. In fact, it is more of an advantage to have someone review and guide you on documentation, and advise you on decisions. Most business decisions have legal ramifications, and it's important to have access to support when an adverse issue arises, and not be scrambling to find someone to help.

2. The structure of your business, when thought about and completed with the right legal protection, will save you much more than the cost of those annual retainer fees, and proper filing of documents.

3. The attorney that I used to close our businesses was one of the best I had interacted with. He provided me with great business advice and helped me to set up another organization that had a financial structure built into it. My biggest mistake was not realizing what he had created for me until many years later. He set up a C corporation for me with the structure to sell common shares to raise money to capitalize my new business opportunity, even though I had ended what was a great set of developments. He had basically guided and advised me to keep doing what I had been doing. He provided me with a new opportunity; I just wasn't ready to see it.

What I Missed: Business Structure and Partners II

I remember the day we closed on the purchase of Downtown Valet Cleaners, and the excitement my mom had when we received the keys to a poorly kept storefront in downtown Pontiac, Michigan, on August 4, 1984. She went right to work the next day; the employee that was managing the operations for the absentee owner stayed with us for a few days. My mom knew all the operational procedures of dry cleaners and only needed limited direction on how to run the business. It was a very exciting time because of the breakthrough of acquiring a business. But the rigors of owning a business caught up with us very fast—things like faulty equipment and a storefront that needed repair became obvious several months after the newness wore off. However, with care and my mom having her alteration clientele, business income increased exponentially.

At the time of writing this chapter, I realized that the biggest structural deficiency was not having set up an organizational chart. I recognize now how many of our shortcomings were internal. Staying in business because it was family was probably the biggest "What I Missed". Trying to manage our businesses without members with upper level management skills on our team that could help grow what we had started was a major missing piece to truly having greater success. No one had been a former CEO, president, CFO, vice president or senior officer in a thriving business. If they had been, they could have brought with them many of the fundamental concepts that could help chart the direction of our businesses. We were limited by our inner circle and our lack of exposure to other business owners that could teach us business concepts for survival and thriving. I remember a CPA from (Follmer-Rudzewicz) we had hired in the later years sharing with me that I had the wrong team members of my family in the business. I appreciated what she shared, but was unable to come up with a way to address these shortcomings. *In fact, I had many of these types of affiliations, but found it difficult to bring this level of individuals to our business. The family team was unable to fit into upper corporate business engagements.*

What I have found in later years is that we were not the exception. With the many small business owners, I've had the privilege of doing business, working for, or working within. I've discovered that many falter in this aspect, so we were not alone in these faults. There are many business owners that I have affiliations with today that I hesitate to introduce to more skilled members of my network, and on many occasions, have made introductions and regret making the introduction.

We were like so many business owners. We wanted the money and fame, but missed out on preparedness for the opportunities when they arrived.

What I learned from many missed opportunities is that getting into a business relationship with the wrong people, even your family members, can be devastating. What I learned was the wrong way to structure an operation.

What I Missed: The Takeaway

1. Be selective of your partner(s), and analyze their strengths and weaknesses. If they are strong in one area, don't be fooled that those strengths can be transferred to other areas. Because they are close family members, you might want to look much harder at all their skills. *For example, I knew my mom was excellent at running the operations of dry cleaners and laundry, but she had zero skills in administration, upper-level business finance, developing a management team, or creating a sales/marketing plan.*

2. It's a hard pill to swallow that the person who is in the lead role in your business is not the best choice. Whether they are your wife, best friend, mom, dad, or favored cousin, have a sit-down with everyone's resumes, and have them make one if they don't have one.

3. Ask yourself the following questions: Does it list managing or growing business revenue to upper six and seven figures? Does it list developing contracts and agreements, along with presenting those to internal or external parties? Have they

managed more than two to five employees? What kind of formal education do they have? Are they okay with sharing or delegating responsibilities? Do they have a vision, and can they communicate it? Are they great team members?

Dealing with people is probably the biggest problem you face, especially if you are in business.

Yes, and that is also true if you are a housewife, architect or engineer.

Dale Carnegie

What I Missed: Know Your Industry

We had baseline knowledge about our industry. My mom had about thirty years of industry experience by the time we opened our first store. She started working for Haspel of New Orleans as a seamstress in her late teens, making men's suits in their Louisiana factory, around the time I was born. She also worked at the local dry cleaners in the town we originated. After relocating to Michigan, she got a job at a dry cleaner and laundromat in Bloomfield Township. She worked for many years managing the evening shift and doing alterations in her alteration shop in her basement, in the evening and on weekends. During those years, she garnered many customers, many I still see occasionally when I return to Pontiac, Michigan. My mom had great operational, technical, and mechanical knowledge about running a dry cleaner, as well as being an ingenious seamstress. I had watched her as a child took a suit apart, used newspaper to make a pattern, and then made a new suit from that pattern. She had a home-based business many years before home-based businesses became popular, in the 1970s. I remember the many customers who would bring their garments for alterations or the making of new garments. I knew when we started the first plan to acquire the operations from her former boss that if the funding could be obtained, it would not be a problem for her to manage the operations. After making the first acquisition, she stepped in like clockwork and started working in the operations. Within one year of being in operations, revenues had increased by 250 percent and had grown by 400 percent the following year.

Having spent about five years in the real estate industry, I had gained considerable knowledge about real estate transactions and used that experience to cobble together the transaction for the purchase of our first store, Downtown Valet Cleaners. I had enough knowledge to get into the business and grow the business an additional few levels. Industry know-how and work experience is a significant part of entering a business startup. If you have these, your learning curve will be minimized because you know the core technical aspects of an operation. My mom had experience at daily opening and closing a dry-cleaning operation, ordering supplies and chemicals of many varying types from her 30 years of experience. She had experienced disgruntled customers; when I observed her deal with an upset customer, I was surprised at how she knew how to stand her ground while maintaining the customer's relationship. She had gained an intuitive approach from her many years of garment care, repair, dressmaking and customer interactions.

What I missed, or ignored was my mom's lack of administrative experience that would help the business to flourish in the next level of development. We accomplished many great milestones in developing five different operations during our time in business; however, the missing experience prevented the exponential growth that was at our fingertips. Having not experienced a higher educational environment, I recognized that the growth perspective from that type of experience was sorely missing in our business ventures. Many of the administrative items that we had difficulty accomplishing or not understanding were in large part hampered by our lack of a traditional education experience. We were very astute people and knew how to function with systems, but having the structure of a classroom setting and eventually a corporate setting to create the team mindset was something we missed in our operations.

Another missed item was leaving my real estate industry experience and devoting all my time to the dry-cleaning industry was not a good action on my part. I mistakenly looked at the real estate industry only from a sales perspective and turned down an excellent offer to go into the appraisal end of the industry. I'm aware that with my growth mentality, I would have achieved the commercial real estate appraisal level. Going into the family business, I stopped engaging in the industry area that I passionately enjoyed, which had given me the knowledge to put the business transaction together in the first place. I got into the real estate business at nineteen years old, creating several milestones that should have led to a great career. I became an accomplished Realtor Associate and Residential Real Estate Appraiser. I did mortgage origination for some years but was never passionate about finance. Even so, I enjoyed putting together business finance transactions because that was money being used to make money.

Another industry experience was an external view from others that I was a natural-born salesperson, which was my enjoyment of sharing with people what I knew and making sure they got what they sought in their purchases. I've held that position for all my thirty-nine years of business and sales experience.

An additional missed opportunity was being affiliated with organizations and not taking advantage of the industry knowledge or the training that was available within them. Two examples come to mind. The first was being a member of the National Federation of Independent Businesses for most of the years we were in business, but never taking them up on their education-based programs that could help our administrative learning needs. The other would be the International Dry Cleaning Institute, which was and still is the leader in the dry-cleaning industry on training, cleaning techniques, and certification. We joined in the early years but didn't keep up the membership, resulting in missing the educational information and affiliation that would have helped the businesses and our team members growing with certifications and training in best practices. These certifications would have helped with giving our staff more managerial training, connected us with other industry leaders, given us exposure to other operators managing multiple business units, and expanded our business mindset.

Having industry knowledge will let you know more about competitors and what you need to compete within your market. We gained considerable knowledge about other dry cleaners when we built our second operations from three shirt laundry accounts to twelve accounts servicing other cleaners in other areas of North Oakland County, Michigan. What we didn't take away from those experiences was all the know-how of what these other operators were and were not doing in their businesses. We had the access but never realized that this was pertinent information we could use in growing our businesses. The cohesiveness of the family members in many of these family-owned businesses was also key, among other aspects.

Another missed area of opportunities was maintaining certifications, licensure and membership in the Local and National Association of Realtors, which I appreciated the knowledge and education I gained from those activities. I was also involved with a local mentoring group as a way of broadening my exposure, but removed myself from these organizations after getting into the family businesses.

What I Missed: Takeaway

1. Even though we were the best in our industry, What I Missed was leaving the industry that I began. Never put all your energy into one project, idea, or business venture, and never leave your first passion.

2. Keep abreast of your industry trends, association affiliations, networking opportunities within your field.

3. Become an expert if possible in more than one skillset, due to changing industry trends and a change or decline occurs in one area, you can transition into another. If competition increases in one area you can position yourself in another. In my experience, the real estate sale and appraisal segments are saturated, the dry-cleaning industry has high barriers to entry, the finance industry is highly regulated and highly saturated. Because of the skills earned in these areas, affords me the opportunity to provide consulting in the small business sector, though there are many business consultants the field is expected to have continued growth until the year 2020 due to the complex environment of business ownership, regulations and management.

Get over the idea that only children should spend their time in study. Be a student so long as you still have something to learn, and this will mean all your life.

Henry L. Doherty, founder CITGO Petroleum Corp.

What I Missed: Business Education

In retrospect, having one session of college classes remaining before receiving a bachelor's degree in Business Administration, I felt for many, many years that higher education and learning was something that I would do after gaining financial and business success. Having spent the last three and three-quarter years in college life, I realized the value that I missed from not having a formal education. Not to downplay the many years spent in the rough-and-tumble of business, it complements my college life experience. What I bring to the class setting is the drive that I have always brought to my work life. Actually, my view of work life is no different when in a classroom experience. In both, you expect to succeed, do your best, and seek the highest reward possible. I stayed out of school primarily because my wife and I focus was getting our son and daughter through college, so work was a necessity to support their education. This discussion revolves around what I missed by not determining how to finish college when I was younger as opposed to doing it now and the impact education had on our businesses, and will have on yours.

Being raised in a household that had not experienced higher education until my generation, had profound implications on my understanding the value of education in general and how it could have made a significant impact on the family businesses. I didn't think that education was important to business because I had not experienced the connection, I didn't think about it a whole lot, but I realize now that my/our lack of formal education affected our earlier business experiences, education can be a profound learning experience that offers knowledge and skills, which would have made significant contributions to the greater success of our family businesses.

Obtaining at a minimum, a two-year degree, would have provided some fundamentals in the basics of writing, reading, math, and higher technical skills, which would have helped with greater problem solving and analytical skills. A four-year degree or at least structured business training sessions would have had profound implications on how we conducted our business affairs, allowing us to experience a wider perspective and a set of experiences other than our limited knowledge of factory and production worker experiences. The education wouldn't necessarily have had to be from a college institution, but a structured learning experience that offered a broader set of life and business experiences that we could have used and would have influenced my mom and some of my siblings to further educational experiences.

Before getting into the family business, seminars and sales training were a way of life for me. If our company had embraced training to learn more about how to manage our operations more efficiently, I know that our outcome would have been more impactful on our family business.

Gaining classroom knowledge on business theory would have sparked a different perspective on our view of items like workflows, understanding vertical and horizontal integration of new operations, problem solving and analyzing data and new systems, looking at our accounting perspective and not just the tax consequences, but managing of business finances on a day-to-day basis, would have had a huge impact. Having experienced human resources, accounting, marketing, and mathematical equations, I realize now how classroom-learning experience, with a shared insight that would have influenced the direction of our businesses. Looking at how to improve our relationship with our employees, policies and procedures, the regulatory environment of our businesses, would have given us greater understanding in dealing with local, state, and federal governments in taxation and licensure. Moreover, courses in business law and human resource law have in-depth information on how we could have protected ourselves in many of the instances we had legal issues by being knowledgeable on who and how to hire professionals.

It's unfortunate how many people in small business don't value education or understand how important education is in their business. In past generations, many small businesses functioned like many large production manufacturers; they hired employees for their hands and backs. In contrast, our new economy hires employees largely for their minds. We took this failed ideology of not valuing education in our family business.

This lack of education being a central part of businesses' growth plans has an influence on why some 85 percent of businesses have major problems of some fashion. The state of Michigan had only 20% of its population holding a four-year college degree from 2000 to 2010. This has a profound impact on businesses and communities being able to compete. Just looking at communities within the state that have populations with members who have degrees greater than 50%, you have more prosperous enclaves. A community that does not have educated members has difficulty attracting businesses that require higher educated people, so that same thing applies to business. A business that does not have educated leaders or leaders that appreciate education amongst its members cannot do a good job of attracting customers and qualified employees that can help grow the operation. Review the Higher Education: Gaps in Access and Persistence Study by Terris Ross of the National Center for Education Statistics, for more information on why and how education may affect your business.

We had expectational customer service and know-how. We knew what we were doing from a production standpoint and we were quite good at it, but we expected those things to win business valor or sustain our existence, and that proved not to be true because we didn't have the other educational components that made thriving in business more profound. Being able to appreciate good information, having a vision/mission statement, being growth-oriented and realizing that 'learning is growing' were aspects that we missed. We also lacked understanding teamwork; we could have used someone giving us guidance on teamwork and why teamwork is valuable as opposed to the hierarchy of a top-down leadership without the skills to grow.

We performed things that we didn't understand. As I mentioned, we did a vertical integration within our company by acquiring a second business to make us more efficient, but we didn't know what it meant. We had literally bought another business, and integrated that business into our system. The intriguing thing we did was shut down components in the new business because we didn't want to duplicate efforts. We knew that we acquired a second dry-cleaning and laundry operation, to supplement our laundry needs because we were smart enough to know that the quality of service that we were getting from a vendor did not satisfy our customers. They were always complaining, and we had to do something to stop the complaining, so that was from a business perspective, ingenious.

What we did not know was how to navigate the waters with expanding our business, and the regulatory issues we created. We needed at least some basic knowledge of what we were getting into: to get the right legal advice, to read documents and see the right type of information that applies to our situation, to make sure that the document represented us or supported us, and if it was the right action in terms of our longevity and ability to finance the new operations.

We had industry associations as mentioned earlier, that we had little or no affiliation, e.g. the International Dry Cleaning and Laundry Institute. We were members of the National Federation of Independent Businesses, and we maintained membership for most of the years we were in business, but we never went to any meetings or trainings. It felt good to see the small plaque every time we paid for the yearly membership fees, but we never went to any meetings to get the exposure and know-how of running a small business.

Again, I'm not trying to downplay many of the great milestones by focusing on the negatives, because we did a lot of great and fantastic things with the lack of formal educational experience. What I am trying to relay is that with the values gained from having an educational mindset, we would have had greater successes. The promotion of education helps in gaining good jobs, but I believe that a good education increases sales and customer service, improves processes, and increases a business' longevity.

In our businesses, we exceeded many of the business norms. The average business doesn't make it to five years; we were around thirteen. Average businesses don't exceed $150,000 to $200,000 in annual revenues, and we grew to between $400,000 to half a million dollars annually, with our sights set on multi-million dollar revenues. We won multiple multi-year government contracts from a customer we held a ten-year relationship, with the largest at $600K, with the opportunity to grow to $1.2 million. We had multiple contracts and agreements with public safety and police departments, municipal, county, and state governmental agencies.

Congressional Act developed the Procurement Technical Assistance Centers (PTAC) in 1985, a year after our going into business, and Small Business Development Centers (SBDC) helped propagate small businesses with assistance in face-to-face consulting, at-cost training in writing business plans, accessing financing, marketing support and insight, guidance on regulatory compliance, directions on import/export trade, and by hosting networking events introducing small businesses to governmental agencies. The interesting thing about SBDCs and PTACs is their connection to universities and college campuses. Attending a higher education institution by a member of our senior team could have potentially exposed us to these entities.

We were involved with governments in contracting purely because they did millions in business each year, and we pursued those agencies and succeeded in gaining opportunities in our skillset. We were ahead of the curve, however this lack of educational experience created missed opportunities.

College education and/or skilled trades training would have provided us with insight into broader areas of our industry. As mentioned, we were a member of the Dry-Cleaning Institute, but we never took that to another level by attending courses or obtaining certifications that would have helped brand our company and given us greater connections in the industry.

We had the information at our disposal, however, with education not being a primary focus in our culture, we never took advantage of it. In our family, we didn't take that next step, so with the experience that I've had today and in retrospect, I see the value of education and the loss associated with not having it in the fiber of our maternal and paternal family's community. I see the mind-changing perspective that an education brings to a businessperson.

I wasn't looking at education from the standpoint of giving me value for my business, but it has given me such an immense amount of value with which to run my business. My view on education in former years was a respect for learning, but today that view has changed to one of lifelong learning.

Being able to communicate with many different type of people effectively is key. I was always able to do that, but now it's with a respect for what they offer (listening), and the value I bring to situations. I've gotten much better at it, and it seems that because of this experiment I'm drawing higher-quality business relations and higher quality of affiliations. The quality was always there, but now I'm more confident in myself in the engagement.

In the networking chapter, I mentioned a relationship with a large group that was helping dry cleaners diversify their business by getting into the uniform and mat rental business, which was an intriguing opportunity for us since we had the large-capacity washers and dryers, that could produce up to 2 million pounds of garments annually, and the warehouse space to expand into that sector. We already had delivery routes, so we were a perfect match—at least I thought so. However, if your team can't see the vision or you can't convey the vision, you probably should not go into the business. Having this relationship with a group of companies that were doing $24 million a year and more, I was looking at stretching the company to a level of doing more business, but I ignored the internal weaknesses, thinking that making the money would solve those problems. What I missed was the need to address those problems before we could experience the added opportunities.

Having exposure to many retail dry cleaning operations and an advisor from SCORE, an SBA affiliation that offers mentorships to startups and existing businesses that need help with development and business strategies, provided much insight in how business functions in small operations and large scale companies. We were involved in many of the right things for growth later in the business; however, struggle and in fighting for more than ten years had drained the excitement out of a great business opportunity.

A survey I observed while on the SCORE's website of one thousand business owners stated that 70% had at least a bachelor's degree.

But having that college education, again, is not the only way to get an education. There are more ways to get an education today other than going to a traditional institution, such as utilizing your association's training seminars or webinars, self-training can be accomplished by companies training their staff to get what they want in a quality education. Trade schools, which have been out of vogue in the U.S. for the last 35 years, can be great educational venues for learning technical skills that lead to great business opportunities. Online training, workshops, seminars and webinars in most facets of business development is available by groups and individual that train business owners and professionals. This book was developed as a training tool of many of our mistakes showing business owners a way to improve.

Again, we had a number of affiliations, but our lack of utilization of those contacts and most specifically training the senior members of our team the methods of managing the businesses and learning new techniques about running a business ultimately harmed us. The education was available, but we were not engaged enough to broaden our leadership's educational experience, which would have influenced us to increase our staff's education, and learn to bring new team member into our organization, and the many opportunities constantly available to us.

I've always felt that the core aspect of running a business is no different from industry to industry, and the type of product or service you provide. The core of it all is the same; you must provide a great product or service repeatedly to every customer, day in and day out, and solve their problems when they arise. Whether it's cleaning clothes or billionaire dollar OEM selling vehicles, you must perform your core functions by exceeding your competitor's offerings and your customer's expectations. To be ahead of the game, one should continue to improve the talent of his or her core team members, and today that means all team members.

But learning and relearning the processes of managing your business, learning new management techniques, finding great mentors, and thought leaders as advisors can help you revolutionize your business. We reached a plateau in our thinking that would not allow us to go to the next level because as one of the leaders, I had exhausted the internal resources and had no idea how to get the next-level team members on our team. I wanted the businesses to go to the next level, but the team was not ready to go to the next level. If your team is not with you, not informed and prepared enough for increased sales and team expansion, or even believe that they can go to that next plateau, you won't get there.

Again, one of the biggest mistakes we made was our not educating ourselves as a group. I was always a proponent of it, but I could not figure out how to get that message to my mom and siblings.

What I Missed: Takeaway

1. Emphatically, I would say to any business owner today, if you have not completed that college degree, go back and complete it. It doesn't necessarily have to be in Business Administration, though I would recommend it.

2. Having a higher education experience puts a structure in your life, develops a committal attitude to follow-through, and creates

great habits of repeatedly doing your assignments as they are due, or dealing with the pressures of getting assignment completed. These are the same experiences you're going to have or having in your work or business life, so why not get some training in a laboratory and the classroom exercises, where there is somewhat less pressure to get the assignment completed.

3. I'm a total proponent of education, and a direct correlation or prerequisite to education is a healthy habit of reading good books that can change your thinking. Reading increases your vocabulary and forms study habits when you must study for quizzes and exams if you are in school or preparing for a certification test or licensing exam.

4. The fundamentals of education have its place in every aspect of your business. I say to any business owner, senior level, entry level or mid level manager in a business or anybody for that matter, read. Read good content, good information. Subscribe to interesting magazines and industry associations in your field. Spend your time reading good quality books that can influence your motivation—increasing your knowledge about a certain technique, product or concept. Self-development should be a central focus in life, it will naturally drive you to develop others.

5. A class experience that gave great value to me and has great value in any organization is Human Relations. It's a class every business owners and managers should take, if they haven't. The class appears to have little value as it relates to business, but what you get out of a Human Relations class is the psychological aspect of human and business relations, so you learn to relate with your employees, relate with your vendors, relate with other business professionals, and relate with customers. And the key thing when you start that class is the assessment of yourself. Many business owners need to know themselves, what their gifts and talents are, but more importantly, knowing what your weaknesses are and accepting those weaknesses so that you can make changes.

6. You can't resolve a weakness by not acknowledging that you have one. By admitting a weakness, you're able to go about

changing it. My view is, weaknesses exist to be changed. It took me a long time to accept and learn how to be engaged with changing my weaknesses. Once I learned that I had to change myself and stop looking for change in others, it became easier to accept others as they are, and if they don't change, had no effect on me, and it became easier for me to make personal changes, which are life-changing. If someone close to you is going the wrong way, you don't have to follow them or get bent out of shape because you know the negative outcome of their actions; you can instead take another direction or keep going on the course you know is best. Learning how to deal with weaknesses was one of my greatest learning experiences, and this class on human relations provided great help with improving my deficiencies.

7. The understanding I got from returning to college as an 'adult learner' was how simple learning is if you want to learn. It doesn't mean you won't have to study hard; it only means you can learn whatever you chose to learn. If you don't know, it doesn't mean that you can't know. If you don't know, it doesn't mean that there's not a way for you to find out. It's up to each individual, the thought leader, and the owner of the organization to find ways to change and grow their business; a learning environment is one of the best methods. Again, I should add that having a lifetime learning mindset is a crucial driving force in growing your business.

8. It's been over thirty-two years since we started our first store and a lot has changed in that time. However, one fundamental that has never changed is the need for a quality education, because it still provides unlimited opportunities and insight. Allow your business to grow by letting learning be a central part of its culture.

Always walk through life as if you have something to learn and you will.

Vernon L. Howard. writer, founder New Life Foundation.

What I Missed: Knowing About Employee Management

Finding good employees is still a challenge today. During the time that we were in business, we had that struggle but thrive with a small core group. However, as we grew and needed more employees, it became problematic. Ours was a situation of operating without the right resources; we didn't have the technology and the administrative talent to manage our human resources effectively. We lacked exposure to other business owners and their best practices. We had no member on our team that had managed a larger-scale business, which I think would have provided us with some of the fundamentals of operations and systems management.

Here are five items I believe would have made a difference in our employee management:

1. Due to a lack of understanding of the need to automate, we failed to make the investment into personal computers, viewing them as expensive and not realizing the value and the need for such a tool for a growing business. We acquired our first computer after being in business close to eight years.

2. Our location had an impact on the quality of employees that were available. Being in an urban environment, we had an influx of undereducated and untrained potential employees.

3. A lack of cooperation among senior management affected our ability to manage the key managers below us. What I will always believe is that not having any examples of bonding in our childrearing years contributed to our lack of being good examples to ourselves and anyone we brought into the business.

4.   We did not advertise, which I think played a part in our lack of quality labor personnel, by expanding the pool of potential staff candidates.

5.   Our location influenced some of our selection options. We were in a central business district with good and bad qualities: we were in the downtown area, but we were off the main road, which limited our exposure by being on a road with marginal commercial traffic.

Obtaining good employees is on most business owner's mind. In retrospect, we had a core of good employees; we just didn't have the understanding and experience within our senior ranks to move the business to the next tier collectively. Most of our senior management did not understand sales and business growth. This was one of our major weaknesses that prevented us from embracing a long-term vision that would create a substantial business legacy 50 to 100 or more years later.

We did not have an issue with work ethic in senior management and line managers; only when dealing with our unskilled labor members did we have staff problems. My contribution to this was not taking my wife's advice to let them go when the work was done and allow family members to work after hours to stay ahead. My biggest weakness was not being able to fire people when the need existed and not having procedures for employees. I didn't realize that there would always be a source of labor, and not to get attached to staff. We were a for-profit, not a non-profit, and we could only truly help those that were willing to help themselves by doing a good job.

Further lack in policy and procedure provided no screening of applicants and ineffective methods to select the good from the bad. I thought this lack of procedure was exclusive to our small world, but after becoming exposed to many small businesses today, it's clear that it is very common for small companies to function without employer/employee protocols. Something that we excelled at was employee relations; however, I find that it is very common practice not to have an understanding of employer/employee relations; it's something that is lacking among many small business owners. Just like us, many small business owners have not put in place any methods of screening employee prospects, policy and procedures, labor and wages regulations, human relations, and understanding the dos and don'ts of interviewing an employee candidate.

Many employers have not studied employment law or even know that they are operating outside of regulatory compliance and can be subject to fines of $10,000.00 and up and audits by many federal and state agencies, per HR consultants and attorneys practicing in human resource law.

Another downside in our business, or another place that exposed us to mistakes in the business, is not knowing how to make good employee selection, myself particularly. Everyone deferred to me on many of our human resource issues, and I lacked the skill set in human resources, it was a definite weakness for our businesses and continues to be a weakness in many small businesses today. *I recently instructed a client on his lack of employment procedures and where he should get help with correcting his actions, after he hired a new staff without an onboarding process.*

One of our biggest employee issues occurred when we hired a gentleman to give him a second chance as a delivery driver of our large delivery truck. We had a couple of instances where he did not show up for work on time. We listened to his excuses and kept him on, even though he had admitted to having drug and drinking problems; stating he had recovered. Some months into his employment, past his probationary period, he started making delivery runs on his own. One day, he left to do a scheduled daily run and did not return. The incident sent everyone into an uproar; we had to inform customers that our employee has not returned from other deliveries and let them know that we would get their orders as soon as the truck was returned. The employee never returned, and the truck was found several days later, still intact, with the customers' product inside. That experience sent shock waves through our business. Still, we had no real way to check out new employees and determine if they were the right choice.

This also showed up in our business during another scenario when we hired a gentleman that was referred to us by a noted political representative, we thought we had an excellent candidate to help our business grow. What we learned was how much we lacked in the infrastructure of our organization around choosing great employees.

Having no knowledge of background checks, we found out after bringing him on board as a general manager and his attempting to take over the business, that he was under court order not to be involved with dealing with any businesses because he had tried to scam a family in Detroit out of their family business. A case had been brought against him, and the judge had found him guilty, and placed him on probation with an order to never be involved with any other business owners. His resume had stated that he was the son of a pastor, and had graduated from Georgetown University. When I approached him about his actions, he went into a rave about my skills. The next day, our computer system was stolen, along with all our data. The irony of this situation was that we had many law enforcement officers that we were doing work for, as well as a member of our family on a local agency staff.

Considering the previous issues, most of our success were derived from having several reliable employees who knew how to manage our operations. We paid them market rates, with no benefits, which many small businesses are still struggling to provide today. However, I always felt that if we could offer benefits that would give our employees some advantages, we would have taken the step. What we could do to the best of our ability was have a good rapport with the employees. I've dealt with many managers who, when I walked into their business, I can feel the negative atmosphere just by the way the employees looked at me in a disrespectful way, and I knew that they had disrespect for their bosses. If employees trust and respect owners and managers they work for, that trust and respect is going to show up in their attitude towards anyone new that the owners bring to the operation, including customers.

Like many other owners of small businesses, we had no policy and procedures. We had no handbook or rules of conduct for management and employees. We attempted to bring in an Aflac agent to give some options for health insurance, however they had to have enough income to support the program. We provided senior staff free cleaning of family clothes as a benefit, along with purchasing of staff lunches on a regular basis, but it was our treatment of our employees who worked for us that, in my opinion, that helped us keep this valued human resource for all the years we were in business.

Some of the missing main points as it relates to employees were items like job descriptions, employee training manuals, employee handbooks, and providing the staff with our workflow or process so that employees could be more efficient. Without these and other tools, we could not build the foundation for growth in our businesses.

With entry-level employees, it was the same thing; a lot of the time, someone else referred someone to us, and we didn't check their background. Again, we really had no medium for checking them out. Our interviewing process was almost non-existent, and as a result, we hired haphazardly, like many businesses continue to do today. Many owners have gotten the training and do very well because the owners have applied their skills from past work experience or use of classroom theory. Others have the background working in their industries for many years for small and large businesses in senior management roles.

What I Missed: Takeaways

1. Not doing background checks, not bringing in an administrative consultant who could have protected us with many of the issues we ran into with employees, not listening to the wisdom and insight from my wife who has always had a way of seeing people's real personalities, and controlled my being too trusting.

2. Services that employers can use today that were not available during our time are professional employer organizations (PEO), who can often provide many of the employment services that a small business need, such as Payroll Administration, Workers' Compensation Administration, Benefit Administration, 401K Administration, background checks, applicant screening and staffing support and much more. Other services might include keeping employees abreast of certification updates or continuing education, if that is needed to stay compliant with licensing and certifications, managing your Workers' Compensation insurance and Unemployment Insurance rates, and keeping your rates aligned with the type of employees that are on your payroll and not having them rated in a higher category.

3. It can help to have a senior member of your small business team with previous and ongoing training in the human resources field.

4. Another scenario introduced to me initially by my son is that of *virtual assistants.* Today, numerous services can be provided virtually online. By using *freelance services,* you can find all kinds of resources to help you with administrative management, marketing your business, building your business plan, and creating, editing or drafting of documents, website design services, audio/video services and much more.

5. Today, you can search the internet and take classes in human relations, human resources, and even classes in psychology to provide your business with the know-how to deal with people in the workplace and all the various personalities that you will engage. Why human relations? Because starting to understand yourself is the first step to understanding someone else.

Ability is what you are capable of doing;

Motivation determines what you do;

and Attitude determines how well you do it.

Lou Holtz, college football most winning coach.

What I Missed: Business Documentation

Looking back on my family's businesses, we did well at completing many of the administrative needs such as filing necessary documents. We filed our business and personal tax returns annually, and we maintained our state and municipal license filings, which are the basic forms of documentation that a business is required to have by legal codes. However, we failed miserably in other areas. Here, I list twelve important documents that we didn't have in our operations, and many small businesses today still have not come to grips with the fact that these pieces of information are necessary to maintain smooth operations.

1. The big one is an **employee handbook,** spelling out how employees are to conduct themselves on the job and the type of employment—at-will employment, employment contracts or independent contractors. Our state employers have an at-will employment relationship, which gives the employer the right to dismiss, hire, promote, or demote any employee he or she chooses within a reasonable manner without notice, and it gives employee the right to leave a job without notice to the employer. Further policies and procedures that may be in a handbook include: conduct on the job, dress code or uniform requirements, rules on tardiness, no-call no-shows, employee/employer harassment, EEOC rules and guidelines, labor laws, job postings, safety in the workplace, drug/alcohol testing, as well as dismissal and termination procedures, among many others. (Check out the Society of Human Resource Management (SHRM), HR magazine or Rocket Lawyer for templates and further understanding).

2. **Employment contracts:** These are usually senior-level staff member agreements best completed by an attorney versed in employment law, addressing types of employment roles,

classification of employment, length of position, roles and responsibilities, a detailed job description, income and benefits packages, etc. (Check out SHRM and Rocket Lawyer for templates and more guidelines.)

3. **Applications:** With the current employment climate and the many things that can get an employer into trouble, I would suggest you go to HR magazine or SHRM for guidelines for employment applications and hire a HR expert or consultant. Many things can't be in an application, from age questions to your country of origin, or who your emergency contact might be; these can lead to possible legal issues. (Check out SHRM's website and HR Magazine, and I would suggest a course in Human Resource Management, you get great information on the details of employment laws.)

4. **Business plan**: A business plan is often viewed as a tool for obtaining business financing. I recommend completing a thorough plan for managing your operations in all aspects, from identifying your mission/vision statements, assessing your management team, development of key personnel, marketing and sales strategies, your financial plan, how you will use the profits generated from your business activities, who your competitors are and how they are impacting your business, demographics, psychographics segmentation, market segmentation, and trends that you might need to develop in your business. A full-scale review of your business should occur at least once yearly, along with comparing/benchmarking your business with the best in class, in your industry. Session planning should be considered with an attorney with strong estate planning and wealth management experience. (Rocket Lawyer offers a business planning template, amoung many others).

5. **Legal entity**: C Corp, S Corp, LLC, PLLC, and others. We functioned as a sole proprietorship for many years primarily

because our leadership did not understand the need nor value of incorporating. With the help of a great business lawyer and CPA, you should have your corporate documents reviewed every couple of years to see if you are getting the best coverage from a liability perspective, and what tax advantages may exist if you form other entities as you grow. Form an operating agreement that lays out the roles and responsibilities of owners, shareholders, and senior management. We established different operations and divisions without the help of legal counsel, and we could have held on to some of those assets if we had separated the divisions into different entities. I got a great lawyer at the end of our development. Get yours now. (A great business attorney can supply you with in-depth information on incorporation, partnership, investor relations, among many other protocols).

6. **Financial statements:** Profit and loss statement, income statement, statement of cash flows, statement of retained earnings, business ratios, among others. Provided by your accountant (CPA) used by the banking and investment industry to determine if a business is a good risk. Courses in accounting are great tools to understanding how your business functions, along with interpreting financial statements. Have your CPA provide training, take a QuickBooks course from a certified trainer.

7. **Lease agreement**: You will need to understand real estate lease agreements and equipment leases. Because of the wear and tear a business can have on a facility, along with changes in building modifications, a landlord will require that your business pays all expenses associated with your space including property taxes, maintenance, and utilities. All upgrades to support your business are your cost. Have a great attorney versed in business law.

8. **Sales agreements, sales contracts, and commission agreements or sales representative contracts:** If you have a sales force or are developing a sales team, one of these agreements might be a better way to define roles, goals, and strategies. Laying out what is expected from your sales staff with a consistent approach will eliminate ambiguity and showing favoritism. Defining territories, customer engagement policies, gifts policies, and expense allowances along with policies that exist in the general employee handbook is important. Look for a great lawyer with labor relations skills if you don't have an in-house HR expert; HR consultants can be great resources that can help with guidance.

9. **Investor agreement:** An agreement detailing the amount of funds an equity investor might invest in your business, receiving an equitable share of company stock or ownership interest. Investor roles can be passive or involved in the operations. If the involved investor brings certain business skills to the operations and the personalities are compatible with the owners, it can be a great resource to help a small business gain a qualified team player without the large upfront expense of a senior manager's salary. The method used to fund 37 percent of small business startups is borrowing from family and friends, per Inc Magazine. Get an understanding of what makes a certified investor. you want to know if they can afford investing, as well as being aligned with Security and Exchange Commission (SEC) and State Financing bureau rules. An attorney and CPA experienced in this area is necessary.

10. **W-9s, W-2s, I-9 forms, 1099**: Do you have a procedure or new employee orientation package with these standard forms and a thorough understanding of your company's responsibilities? See an HR expert and/or a PEO company for directions.

11. **Letter of intent:** Can be created by your attorney for submission in outlining intent to make a major purchase, intent to provide financing, or deliver a proposal to perform a service. See Rocket Lawyer for templates or talk to your attorney.

12. **Customer sales contract:** There are many types of agreements that relate to the type of business you are in. From experience, I would recommend against developing your own due to the need to have proper language in your agreement that protects your business interest if nonperformance or a breach occurs. Have your attorney develop a generic contract that can be used with most of your customers with areas for modifications, changes, and upgrades.

What I Missed: Business Document Takeaways

1. The most important need is having a method to acquire resources and advisor that can help you navigate all your business functions from entry stage to growth stages of your enterprise.

2. Therefore, the value of reading and learning is so important, if you as an owner have a problem that become a major issue that results in a fine, lawsuit and judgement, you will be held fully accountable. Reading can help with understanding what you get into along with understanding your advisors.

3. Have an assessment of your current documentation needs, a list of how long certain documents should be saved and how they are saved needs to be addressed. Storage and disposal of pertinent document procedures. Who has access to your files as well as privacy must be addressed.

4. A human resource class as a starter can be of great benefit, check HR magazine for resources, online there are many choices, do careful research within your network. Joining the Society of Human Resource Management will give you great information.

5. Interviewing Profession Employer Organizations (PEO) will provide a storehouse of resources, guidance, services and protection if you use them. We work with DEM Group and area PEO firm, call us if you want to make contact.

Xerox is really good at managing documents, and we're definitely good at managing through a process.

Ursula Burns, Xerox CEO and Chairman.

What I Missed: Legal Issues

During our last year in the family business, I found a lawyer that was interested in giving me advice that was worth the fees he charged. He had a business background that we could have used in every aspect of our business's life. The second attorney we hired for a case blew it and cost us $14,000.00 and a judgement, the result of not knowing how to select the right legal practitioner, one who had an interest in his client's wellbeing. The greatest sentiment that I have for lawyers is that most that I have engaged will not give advice for the benefit of their client; they can only think of a suit as an answer to any issues as oppose to negotiation and mediation.

For every case, we engaged, we selected the wrong attorney due mostly to not knowing that a general practitioner does not have enough real estate or business experience to give his client the right direction. Case in point, we sued the former owner of our second operation for hiding the conditions of the building we purchased (caveat emptor), inclusive of paying kickbacks to city inspectors on buildings conditions. We had an open-and-shut case; however, our attorney of choice missed the preliminary exam to explain our case, causing the judge to dismiss our case. It was the most infuriating time that I have ever experienced when hiring someone. His response was that we didn't have to pay him the fees, but compared to having a judgment entered against us by the seller that sold us a building that had been neglected and had covered up the neglect with the help of city inspectors, it wasn't much comfort, along with loss of a thriving business we had developed.

In another case, we had an eminent domain action taken by the economic development director for the city we were located. We had survived within the city when everything was economically down. When the initiative was spearheaded to revitalize the area, some of the existing businesses were not given the opportunity to acquire vacant buildings for a dollar, which had been offered to out-of-town bar and restaurant prospectors. We were given ninety days' notice to relocate with no assistance, yet we had paid taxes and struggled with our business in the city. Many owners had been in their businesses for more than fifteen years. The attorney we selected was well known in town, so we felt he would do the right thing. However, we found that he wanted to file a class action suit, which we couldn't agree with. Considering that we could not sustain a court battle with a municipality that had a $170 million budget, we preferred to negotiate. Counsel disagreed with our viewpoint and wanted to force us into a long-term litigation; again, counsel had the resources to navigate this legal process, but as a client, we knew we could not focus on our business and fight a case at the same time. we fired the attorney, dealt directly with the city, and negotiated a relocation agreement that provided funds for a new plant relocation, rehabilitation and equipment.

Maybe we just had no experience in selecting lawyers; however, most of my engagement with legal professionals has been with parties that when I was completed with whatever issues, I had no interest in ever dealing with the legal profession again. The word 'counsel' is an oxymoron when you deal with many in the legal profession; many times, they do not counsel, but instead come up with ways to justify their fees and never give advice that would benefit their clients. Again, this view comes from my personal experience and is not applicable to everyone in the legal profession that is doing a great job for their clients.

The gentleman mentioned at the beginning of this section was the most informative and inspirational legal professional I've met that represented me. I have found others in the profession over the years who have the same character. Though I have been very critical of attorneys, there are many respectful professionals in the industry; this is *what I missed* while operating our family enterprises, and I think that if we had a good legal professional earlier in our business ventures, our longevity would have been greater.

What I Missed: Takeaway

1. What I want you to take away from our experience is to make it a priority to find a great legal counselor. Make a list of your business needs and go shopping; interview four or five different counselors with a business background.

2. Ask close business acquaintances for attorneys that have experience with knowledge in business, estate planning, real

estate acquisitions, and finance backgrounds, they have worked with in the past.

3. Make it a priority to create a budget line item for retainer fees.

4. Do a check with the county and state bar associations, and check out the judicial grievance boards in your state to see if a legal professional has had complaints filed against them.

5. As with all aspects of your business, do your due diligence; it always pays to do some checking around. Do not repeat our experience by using the popular law firm and ending up with the wrong counselor with no real business background or client interaction skills.

The more informed you are,

the less arrogant and aggressive you are.

Nelson Mandela.

"When the trust account is high,

communication is easy, instant and effective"

Stephen Covey

What I Missed: Marketing

Having spent thirteen-plus years in our family business and having many highs and lows in that business experience, I realized that having a background with some degree of product and service marketing or experience with the 5 P's of marketing (positioning, packaging, promotion, persuasion, and performance) would have been very beneficial to us and helped us to achieve even greater success in our business experiences. What we knew was that location was most important, but having access to a better location comes with a cost for a startup with minimal access to capital; we started where we could. Packaging requires some knowledge and experience about the process—who do you go to in order to create a high-quality package, and for us, understanding the value of such packaging (image of our service, storefront, plant, operation, and vehicles). Regarding promotion, we did as much marketing as our humble finances would permit (Yellow Pages ads, local news publications, and the proverbial word of mouth, which gave great results, because the quality of our work was very high). Persuasion had no place in our consciousness; we felt we offered a great service and felt no need to persuade someone to purchase from us, not realizing persuasion is an important component in future sales, (i.e. selling additional services, asking for referrals, and recommendations), Performance is where we excelled; we created one of the best teams in the marketplace.

We used the services of a local public relations expert, who helped with the branding of our print materials and a few marketing pieces. Creation of handbills and flyers was often done by hand or created with the support of a couple local print shops.

We were like many small businesses who understood the value of marketing, but getting it accomplished was always an uphill battle when wrestling with cash flows while growing our operations.

As stated earlier, we had access to resources through our affiliation with a business advocacy group, but never took advantage of the opportunity because we lacked an understanding of the value and to some extent, because of fear of asking for help. We often don't want to look unintelligent by asking questions about things we think we should already know.

We used an extensive amount of direct selling and networking with our contacts, which led to most of our expansion opportunities.

Again, the shortcoming of lacking a formal business education meant that we hadn't gained the knowledge we needed to understand that we were on a great path, but needed the resources and access to the overall community to really excel.

Developing a formal marketing plan was an idea that never left the pages of our business plan because we primarily did not understand the value of well-financed marketing efforts, even though we continued to embark on marketing efforts such as approaching purchasing departments, creating relationships, and winning multi-year contracts for processing garments and uniforms. Two of the milestones we achieved was growing contracts revenues from $300 weekly to $4,500 weekly over a six year period and after acquiring our second operation and restructuring that business unit. We improved an operation that functioned at a 10 percent efficiency level up to a 75 percent efficiency level. This involved improving production processing from 300 shirts per week, to processing 500–700 shirts per day, a 1000 percent improvement over 18 months, with constant external threats and opposition. The method to our success included pre-spotting and scrubbing the cuffs and collars of laundered shirts before washing and blowing the wrinkles out after the shirts came off the shirt pressing unit; approaching medical offices and offering our delivery program; opening a retail outlet in an upscale business and tech community; internally processing customer orders to the highest industry standards; and growing customer relations from our multiple bid awards. Without a formal marketing plan, the marketing of our business functioned in earnest.

What I have found is that many small businesses suffer from the exact same maladies we were exposed to: limited internal business knowledge, no exposure to firsthand examples of how a business should be managed, and misguided leadership skills.

In 2013, I restarted my formal education and realized after enrolling in courses on entrepreneurship how much I have learned without a formal education. I finished the first two years graduating Magna Cum Laude with a 3.89-grade point average. What I learned was how truly successful our family businesses had become and how education could have been instrumental in completing the next transition that we consistently developed but could not complete. We had an aspect of marketing that we did very well, which did not show up in the marketing courses, which was marketing to our internal staff. What I learned in our businesses was that having great relationships with your employees made for great relationships with our customers, and we could do that well.

I continue to realize that we missed many marketing opportunities, like not getting signs on our trucks, which would have given incredible exposure when making deliveries to the forty-two different customer businesses and governmental agencies we supplied services. This would have been an excellent opportunity to offer our services to the communities we had expanded our services to and given us a chance to grow sales.

Finding ways of investing more dollars in our storefronts making them more appealing was another missing component to greater successes.

Another missing area was having senior members on our team that could appreciate the opportunity of having a partner that had $24 million in revenues and operational resources, who was working with us to expand into the laundry and uniform rental business.

From a marketing perspective, we knew our customers because we had handled processing of garments with 12–13 other dry cleaners, so we had great insight on how they functioned, but did not know the value of that knowledge or how to convert it into more significant revenue.

What I Missed: Marketing Takeaways

I recognize this more emphatically today, dealing with so many small business owners who struggle with getting to the next-level growth of their businesses. The answers are not easy. However, there are the best solutions to help you get to the next step of your business development.

1. We often end up in business with no real plans, so it's vital to create a plan before you get started, to do it after starting makes growing your operations harder than it must be. One of my present business mottos is 'failure to plan, is planning to fail."

2. Consider who your partners are, who your key team members are, and their strengths and weaknesses. When I helped, my mom start the first through the last business units, I was focused on solving a specific set of problems; her gaining income, not the more important function of how we managed and shared roles.

3. Should I have been in the business with my mom, and should I have demanded more control earlier on? If the senior partner wants to control but has no administrative or marketing skills, this should have been my queue to go in another direction.

4. My biggest mistake was continuing to be the key player in marketing and growing a business that I had no real ownership or control in the early stages of development.

5. Not having a backup plan; I left my backup plan when I stopped my involvement in the real estate industry, with multiple skillsets and in many instances applying marketing and sales techniques.

6. Again, that 'reading' thing keeps coming up; class in marketing, branding, sales and promotion will be great resources and is a key administrative part of a highly successful business. Make marketing a study for your business future growth, by keeping abreast to industry trends, along with changes in consumer habits and expectations.

Competition brings out the best in products
and the worst in men.
Author Unknown

What I Missed: Networking

My early experience in real estate was because of taking classes at Oakland Community College, paying out-of-pocket for a degree in real estate science while working for a concrete pipe company; first as a laborer and eventually as a machine operator. After being laid off from that position, I wanted to continue attending school for my degree. I approached the counselor for help but was informed that there was nothing that could be offered. Receiving misguided information from the school's counselor and not listening to my girlfriend (who ended up being my wife, and was in college at Oakland University), I decided to study for licensure as a real estate agent. After self-study for about three months, I took the real estate exam through Educational Testing Service at Oakland University and passed the first time. At nineteen, I was a licensed real estate agent. I placed my license with a local broker agency in town. After one year, I relocated my license with the help of a fellow agent, to Drayton Plains, Michigan. That is when networking became a part of my ongoing career. After a number of years, having grown a modest business following, I gained enough knowledge to realize that I needed some form of income diversification, while observing and working with agents and brokers around me who were developing land, doing high-level real estate trading, buying and flipping homes, acquiring and selling businesses, or were owners and partners in various businesses and partnerships. I had limited second-hand exposure to networking and how deals were constantly being made, largely based on past relationships and reputations in the local community.

So, having gained this basic knowledge and knowing the limitations of my family's household, the incentive to strive for greater income in an environment that conducted business in this fashion as a way of life influenced my decision to say yes when my mom was offered the opportunity to buy the business she worked for $150,000.00. I approached some financing organizations with no success. One year later after the business was sold, my mom had to find other work, which she had a hard time adjusting to due to the management role she had with her former boss. An ad was posted in the *Oakland Press* for dry cleaners for sale for a great price. We made an appointment, viewed the site, and decided to find a way to finance the purchase. By taking out a second mortgage on my mom's home and asking a cousin to invest $10,000, we bought the business for $10,000 down and a purchase money mortgage on the balance of $10,000, which was paid off in eighteen months. I used many of my affiliations from the real estate industry to close the sale, including using my broker as the closing agent. I used my network to help complete the sale, going to the attorney I used to refer real estate customers to for review of closing documents, and our title insurance agency.

Networking has always been a part of my business experience. There have always been connections that I have made because of an affiliation or an introduction. What I had experienced through the years is how these connections have been able to grow primarily from a premise I believe to this day: Give your best to the persons you get the opportunity to do business with, no matter how small or large the transaction. Giving it my best continues to be the best method today. Have I been disadvantaged with this approach? Yes, I can name numerous scenarios where my helping approach was taken advantage of. However, I can name countless other relationships where my putting all my efforts in for a client or customer has generated enormous rewards, multiple referrals, and repeat business. So, my methodology for networking is to give great service to the person in front of me. If they are the right person, they will reward you by sharing the great experience they had with you, with their friends, family, and very close associates.

This networking thing that is all the rage today has great benefits, but if you approach the development of building your business around a premise of great service, your network grows exponentially. I have countless experiences of getting multiple referrals and repeat business because of my intent to give my best effort, my intent to do right by the person(s), and to do what I promised even when it may not be in my best interest, but it is of theirs.

Our family business existed despite our weaknesses, lack of resources and understanding, which was based on the premise of giving great service. We were able to build a network of customers in unusual circumstances, like taking a contract that was next to impossible to get revenue out of and making the service overly convenient, by adding a delivery service to all of the customers and officers in six locations in the contract, which allowed us to add customers because the relationship from servicing the first group of customers grew to other groups in the area.

Some of my bigger mistakes included leaving a network of relationships I had developed over a decade in the real estate industry, not maintaining those connections, and not continuing the use of the skills and knowledge I had gained. I looked at the negative aspects and not the positives, such as the achievements made in many adverse times. I think I downplayed my gifts to be aligned with my mom and siblings; in retrospect, it was not the right thing to do for my nuclear family.

Other mistakes include building great relationships but letting the family business influence my personal development. As stated in the chapter, "What I Missed – Fears," having spent seven to eight months as a field real estate appraiser, I was offered the opportunity to move to Adrian, Michigan, to work for a thriving father-and-son team in that community. I turned down the offer for many reasons, believing that my family members could not continue running the operations without me interceding in the many problems the business faced.

As mentioned earlier, I was being offered the chance to build a relationship with a senior member of a major local employer, but due to limited thinking, I felt I could not service her to the level she needed because of the demands of the second operation we had started. Eventually, I altogether gave up on the real estate industry because of a lack of understanding of the value it had brought me. I didn't realize that I needed to maintain this income stream because, though often sporadic, it created many significant windfalls.

I walked away from the many buyers and sellers I had conducted business with, leaving those opportunities to gain repeat business as well as referred business. The businesses network grew while I let my personal network languish. While I was involved in the family business, I completed several corporate transactions with a Mr. Robert Dewey, who I've mentioned later as a mentor, who was a former CFO of Chevrolet Division as well as the financial genius behind Delorean Motor Car Company's financing. Bob became a close associate after we completed several creatively financed real estate and business transactions together.

Though there was plenty of opposition in learning the real estate business, I gained considerable skills and reputation, however, I walked away from a great resource for my own personal household, as well as the many transactions I had become so well versed in performing. I turned away from many successes, such as becoming a top agent in the state of Michigan for a national franchise.

I think the greatest drawback to my networking abilities was not being able to make it connect within the business fully. I knew a considerable number of people but felt I could not formally introduce them to the family enterprise, primarily because we never could have the business represent itself as a class business. Again, we did great work, but understanding the value of a competitive image was not something my family fully embraced.

As a group, we didn't fully understand the importance of networks and how they influenced business growth. I was invited to attend monthly events of county-level businesses, but never took up the offer from the Chief Administrator of Oakland County Purchasing Division, because I felt we could not represent a thriving organization and lack of confidence. Even though we made significant accomplishments, we never excelled in image and brand, things that my mom didn't really understand.

Today, networking is a way of life for many businesses, and through it they are gaining great benefits. As an example, if you are in the right BNI networking group, you can earn great rewards if you bring an excellent service and can stay up with their weekly meeting's demand. I have been personally invited by a former client and affiliates to multiple events, as have many other businesses, and think they are great resources for opportunities. I am a member of a significant group in central Oakland County, Michigan, that offer great events monthly and has great partners that are major business owners and professionals. I have a direct affiliation with a local wealth manager that connects me to their network and I in turn have connected them to members of my network, working to connect resources for multi-million dollar projects. All my present business is a result of referrals for networking contacts or former business relations.

When dealing with clients, one of the mainstays of my services is connecting clients when they can use the resources within my list of close contacts. If the relationships can be beneficial and the parties have integrity, show sincerity, and conduct business in an honorable manner, I will consider making an introduction.

What I was guilty of was the fear of showing the weaknesses of my family team members in our organization to the many high-level connections and business associates I knew. I don't know the right answer to this condition, and I'm sure other businesses struggle with this scenario. In hindsight, I would recommend that if your business associates and partners are reasonable, try to get them to see the value in personal improvements and improving the business's image. This may sound a bit rude or capricious, but knowing what a great presentation looks like, I knew that our image was subpar and that risking introducing someone would do more harm than good, so I opted not to create an embarrassing situation.

In my current role as a consultant, if the client is not up to speed on their business etiquette, financial skills, or just don't understand the importance of creating relationships, I will back away from making an introduction. I take care in making introductions because of the value I place on each person being introduced. If a connection is unprepared, I would rather guide them on getting prepared than make an introduction and know that the image will turn the key person off.

The value of networking is intrinsic. I take an internal approach both with myself and the view of the client from their capacity and sophistication. This means that you must have some sense of what the parties need, their position, and their level of business before making an introduction. This is not a guarantee that the connection will be a fit, but at least consideration is given to the compatibility of all who are concerned. Today I am very selective of my networking activities because of ongoing classes and a number of clients I am representing. However, with the many contacts I've had the opportunity to engage, networking continues to take place.

Just like there is art to being connected to the right customer or client, I believe that networking is more of an art. I am usually looking for two to three compatible business owners that can appreciate what I offer and can see the benefit of our getting together. If the match feels and appears right, then a more formal introduction will be made to determine if there is something we all can benefit from.

What I Missed: Marketing Takeaways

Networking is a very important part of conducting business today. A business owner can't just stick their head in the sand because they have a great product; that product must be introduced in the most creative fashion possible. Networking is one of many tools a business owner should use.

Do as much background checking on the group you are looking at joining as possible, as well as be ready to be checked out yourself.

Find a great group and offer great products, services, and content.

Get help with branding your company, your first impressions are your last.

Look at marketing as an investment, you don't have to manipulate customers to do business with your company, just be authentic, straightforward and sincere.

I've learned that people will forget what you said,

people will forget what you did,

but people will never forget how you made them feel.

Maya Angelo

What I Missed: Finding a Mentor

When I reflect on my past, I've had many relationships that can be viewed as mentorships. What I've found, though, was that in some instances, these mentors did not have my best interest at heart. Much of what I learned from these experiences, and many of those whom I call mentors didn't know that they were mentoring. Starting with my granddad, I spent all my early childhood years with him on his farm, and as I write this, I really miss not having spent my teenage and early adult years with him. He was not an educated man; school was not allowed for folks from his background, and being part African American and part American Indian as the story was told, he received little to no schooling. What I remember and still admire about him and my grandma is their work ethic, their persistence, and their commitment to God and family. The other thing I remember is how effectively they had learned to manage their farm, plant seeds, cultivate the crops, harvest the produce, sell the harvest to the local cooperative for delivery to markets, and use the excess for family and neighbors. There was always an abundance of food and work on our farm.

What my siblings, our cousins, and I received from our grandparents was this indelible ability to work. What I got was this ingrained ability to understand entrepreneurship, having lived with people that practiced entrepreneurship in its rawest form and didn't even know it.

What I missed was the full transferal of my grandparents' knowledge, largely because their children didn't know or could not fully see what they had: a commodity that is always in limited supply (land) and the ability to fill a need (food). For me, my granddad was my first mentor. Though he was not educated, he set examples that I continue to live by today. Though he was not perfect and had many flaws, I continue to marvel at the great things he provided. He was married to his childhood sweetheart for close to seventy years until he passed at about ninety years old, raising and providing for eleven children, who have raised ninety-nine grandchildren. Many follow my grandparents' example, as I do; we are hardworking, committed to family, and take honor in providing quality in our work experience. I was raised predominantly by my grandparents, so I got a lot of stuff that some of my siblings and cousins did not, my creativity came from this experience.

The other experiences I had with mentorship was haphazard; I was not left with much direction from my engagement with older members of my family, community, and not the local business community. I had a growth mentality from early childhood and has existed all my adult life. I've had engagements with many people; some of these relationships have remained for many years and are still strong even though we don't often get a chance to visit or spent time together. My childhood experiences with a mentor or example of an adult male was with my grandfather, who was a farmer by trade, as mentioned. As a young person, I didn't appreciate what I learned from growing up around him; however, the fundamental values that I live by today were harvested from the days spent watching my granddad until age fourteen. As a child, I mostly dreamed of getting away from the small farm life, however, today I miss the open spaces, the value of hard work, the experience of watching crops grow in their seasons, and bringing the bounty to our home on that obsolete wagon with two mules, some forty years after the automobile had gained popularity and the common man had access. I dreaded those days when we had to travel out to the main highway to our home from the fields and have cars speed by.

After many years and now knowing what effect not being allowed an education and living through the Great Depression had on my family's history, I now admire their frugality. As a youngster, I devalued those experiences on the farm, not realizing how much value I'd obtained until I had spent many years in adult life.

My strong work ethic, achiever personality, creative mindset, and ability to stay committed to a goal or relationship were all developed as a child growing up with my grandparents. The principles taught by my granddad comprise some of the best mentorships a young boy could receive. As a fifteen-year-old and throughout my teenage and early adult years, I sought the exposure to a good example of a male role model; I always wonder where this thought came from until it occurred to me that my early childhood experiences with my granddad planted the seed to seek such an example. I hadn't realized that he was a mentor to me even though he was not able to explain what he provided. I understand now why it was so hard to leave the farm and that the longing for an example had been fulfilled far greater than it had for many young males I grew up with.

Growing up on a farm laid the groundwork for the immense amount of business knowledge I have accumulated over the years. It came from the experience of watching my grandparents grow crops, which were always bountiful all the years I grew up. Those experiences influenced the intense amount of knowledge and application of business in my work life. If I didn't understand a certain skill, I was trained to work hard at learning a task and to become proficient at it. This came from my grandparents' example.

I remember vividly the large sack of cotton seeds soaked in fertilizer sitting near the pantry on the back porch, waiting for my granddad to fill his mule-drawn planter and move along the long rows of plowed beds in our cotton fields. I remember being taught how to chop cotton and having a sack made to fit me for picking cotton, or the planting, chopping, and pulling of corn for most of my childhood life. As a youngster, I hated the hard work; however, as an adult, I respect and appreciate those values today. I was taught an independent life. My grandparents worked for themselves, so I had limited exposure to someone working a job to make a living for their household until I was fourteen years old. By this time, it was a part of my character to live this way, and it was the best example I could have received from my grandparents, and my granddad particularly.

After getting into adulthood, I still longed for a positive example. Many interactions with adult males in my community were bad examples that were taught by many generations of bad examples. Most of my experience was driven by the limited exposure to my granddad, and wanting something different from what was in my community. I understand today that outside influences created many things in life and that the adults had little or no control of their life directions. But there were a few that were exceptions, and somehow, I got that chance. As I grew older, I intimidated most of the older men in our community. I had gotten a real estate license by nineteen, been a top-producing agent by twenty-four, put my mom in business by twenty-five, and was the main contributor to expanding the family business five times by thirty-five. Most of my experience was lonely because most of the males around me had little in common with someone that loved reading and structuring business transactions.

At around 27, I put a real estate transaction together that impressed a gentleman, as mentioned earlier, Bob Dewey, who was an executor of an estate, and a retired CFO for a division of General Motors. Bob structured the finances for a new automobile manufacturer. To me, the project we worked on was very complex to someone with limited exposure to the real estate industry; it required knowing how real estate finance tools worked and using those tools to address complicated issues. This one was: "How do you finance the purchase of a condemned home, with a buyer that does not have cash?" Some fundamental questions needed to be asked, such as, what are their plans for the property? Do they have credit and an employment history? Are there other tools that can be used to solve the problem? I recognized the answer to all the questions the minute I had a conversation with all parties. I had to do some quick research to determine if one factor would work, which I call the 'linchpin' to the problem, and that was whether the buyer could get a construction loan that would allow the condemned home to be demolished and a new foundation be dug and a deck built, and be paid for out of the first construction draw. Once this was confirmed, I knew I had solved the problem. I only needed to communicate it to all parties. We were successful in taking a condemned home and using a common finance method to change the property from non-conforming bank finance conditions to conforming bank finance conditions, making the transaction fit banking guidelines. We used a land contract to get the buyers in ownership of the property, a construction loan to solve the issue of elimination of the condemned property since the buyers wanted a new home built, and finally, a permanent mortgage to pay off the construction loan and give the new homeowner their long-term mortgage agreement.

After guiding the finance of the condemned house, Bob requested help with financing a CAD CAM computer system, for a tier 2 supplier in Almont, Michigan, and followed that with the need to raise funds for a leverage buyout. Bob and I embarked on helping other business owners with financing their deals. He helped me to realize how much I knew and exposed me to parties I had no idea lived in the community near my hometown—for example, owners of the Buhl Building in downtown Detroit, a developer of apartment communities in the Northville/Novi area of Michigan and in Florida, as well as a former president of Ford who was a general manager at GM, and later a president of White Motors. I still possess some of the documents to those transactions. Again, this was not a formal mentorship; however, I gained a lot of insight being exposed to Bob Dewey. This was like many acquaintances that saw the gifts that were planted in me while growing up on an out-of-the-way farm in southern Mississippi. What I learned from Bob was the magnitude of how large transactions could be structured. I had a sense of who Bob was, but it did not sink in that he was ahead of Chevrolet division finance and structured the deal for DeLorean Motor Car company, along with many other large-scale finance transactions. I often asked why he brought this number of business deals to me to help fund. The part that was oftentimes missing was getting the inside knowledge of how business transactions are developed at the ground level, so again, I could not say it was a real mentorship.

My studious and persistent character often worked against me. Many leaders were intimidated by my knowledge and skills, which was predominantly my stick-to-it mentality. I often spent most of my time alone, crafting deals and projects in the many positions I held through the years.

The next person I viewed as a mentor was a business owner whom I spent many years visiting at his apartment communities. In the early years, I admired this gentleman for building his business to some 800 plus units. Our relationship started with me solving a problem with a project they had purchased in the large retailer I worked for. After many years of visits and discussion of issues about his family businesses and my usually coming up with suggestions to solve problems in conversations, I started to share advice from my many years in my family's businesses and my years of real estate and business transactions. I would get introductions to his business acquaintances, but in retrospect never to work directly in his family businesses. When the business troubles started to get out of control, my natural inclination was to help, but with some form of income for the support I offered. I made suggestions like applying for the DTE energy saving program to replace boiler systems in their buildings and upgrade other items that would have large savings in utility cost.

They would take advantage of the free stuff, but could not think of a way to make an investment into a building that would generate a 40 percent savings on utility cost and give them greater cash flow for the long term. I suggested a method to raise money from a cash flowing indirect asset; the first suggestion on improving mechanical systems would have saved over $100,000 annually. The second suggestion did generate over $300,000 in capital from an asset acquired from a building purchase; however, the advice was treated as if it had no value. I always believed that his family was responsible for taking my advice and not respecting or wanting to pay for the great information. However, some years later, while arranging financing and a team that could help them prevent the loss of their businesses, I began to realize that he was as much as his family was against paying for the services I offered and in a number of cases provided great help.

I was approached again several years later to engage him and his family. I put up front what I did in my business, and the response was that they could not afford to hire me, but wanted me to help them resolve some problems with a number of potential million-dollar real estate transactions, I kindly declined. It took me some time to realize that this relationship was always one-sided. I admired his success, but recognized that there was no room for my success in this relationship. After declining and choosing to be more proactive about reaching out to better quality prospects, the quality of clients I worked for in my business increased. What I gained from this relationship was a lot of knowledge about what not to do again. I also gained other relationships that contributed to the writing of this book. I'm still engaged with the team that I pulled together to help this business owner reorganize his businesses. Though his key family members and attorney did not believe that the team had what it took to help them. These key partners that saw my worth completed the funding of a $63 million plus transaction that was at the scale of what this business owner's family was attempting to do but failed.

What I missed in this presumed mentorship was that I was being taken advantage of and that my kindness was viewed as a weakness. I learned a lot from the experience, most importantly that many people feel that what you must offer should be given to them for free, allowing them to make great returns from your knowledge and hard-earned skills, while you just get by.

Noticing the issues that occurred in my family businesses show up in this family's businesses, should have given me enough insight to back away, but I maintained an attitude of trying to help. I learned that you can't help selfish and self-centered individuals, and much of the same stuff was in my family. What I attribute part of our failure to was our lack of bonding at an early age, and what I recognized in this family's business were the same elements, where no one considered anyone but themselves.

The next relationship is more of a business partner that treats me like a family member. There is mentoring that takes place due to his more than forty-five years of experience in the automotive industry. We had similar struggles in business, having lost businesses and having been in bad relationships. What I get from this relationship is that I met someone with a similar transparent attitude about business, who is a hard worker and strives for excellence. The funny thing about our relationship is that the person that introduced us has been purposefully removed from relationships and association with either of us, based on different circumstances but the same type of selfish actions. What is interesting is that I advocated for this party we both no longer have relations, when we were first introduced.

We have our differences, but they are always talked through and worked out. He has done some intriguing things, like introduce me to high-level auto executives, like my exposure to Bob Dewey. He held leadership roles in a large tier-one OEM suppliers, he has introduced me to lifelong business associates, and we work on large-scale business projects. Our relationship is still intact, and I am most appreciative of the transparency and finally meeting someone that I am comfortable with as a business associate, mentor, and friend.

What I have begun to appreciate about the gifts that come so naturally to me is owning my value. I've stopped being afraid to ask and now expect a reasonable value for what I offer, which is usually life-changing for the business owners I do business with. My son, who watched and worked with me all the thirteen years in the family businesses, has spent many of his adult years pushing me to acknowledge my gifts and to place a value on them aligned with the value I bring to business owners I engage.

The mistake that I made is not realizing that he had his own observations of me and could see me much better than I could see myself. What I have been able to recognize now is that I was his mentor, and did not think of it that way. Actually, both my son and daughter mimic many of my ways, work habits, ethics, strive for excellence, and have a love for reading. Despite myself, I became a mentor to my children. Though I long to do more, their development has been my greatest accomplishment. In my quest to find a mentor, I ended up being one myself, with flaws and all. In this next life, as my wife calls it, my goals are to continue setting examples for my son, daughter, daughter-in-law, granddaughters, and the community(s) I live in.

What I Missed: Takeaway

1. Get away from personalities the moment you notice that they are only interested in themselves and no other people. Usually, the signs are there; just be willing to admit to yourselves what you see, and not be jaded by the potential income you think you might make.

2. Another missing perspective was the need to look inside myself for the example I could not find as a young man. I want to inspire other young and old persons that if you are seeking a positive person in your life, and can't find them, then you must become that person. This example will be of grave benefit to you, your family, customers, community, and legacy.

3. This is not always easy, however, look for examples that resonate with who you are, that make your contribution to your family, community and particularly your children positive ones.

4. Even if you are young, you may have to be the example, I struggled with this for many years, because of the belief by society that the older ones are the most responsible and should be the leaders. I have found that can be grossly false, if you have sincere qualities that can help someone, you are required to help, lead, and mentor.

5. When I reflect on my community of my teenage years and found few examples of positive role models, I'm finding today the same exist in our overall society, that there are very few positive male roles models, so inherently if you are looking for these examples, you might have to become one yourself. For those of you that are setting examples in your homes and communities I commend you!!!!!!!!

"Our chief want in life is somebody who will make us do what we can."

Ralph Waldo Emerson.

What We Missed: Business Advisors

L ooking back over the history of our family business, one of the things that we lacked was good advisors, circumstances that is still commonplace with many small businesses today. However, with the advent of the Internet, access to information and advisors' resources are a lot easier to obtain, and as a result, the playing field is being leveled for small business owners to tap into resources and advice, to help them with business dynamics. When we started, we gained an advisor through a bank relationship at our infancy stage that changed over the years. When we did our second project, our growth was not accepted as the norm in our community. We ignited a negative sentiment among local leadership; I think largely because of a lack of understanding about growing diverse business groups. With this project, we had no advisors to tell us what to do or what not to do, such as assist us with a strategy for dealing with municipal leadership. Our increased engagement with local governmental agencies, worked against us, causing us to focus on political bureaucratic rather than on growing the business.

After doing a buyout of another fledging business our financial picture declined, this second acquisition didn't turn out as well as we had anticipated. The problem was mainly due to our lack of understanding of business planning, partly to the political environment, the location of the business and the building's conditions.

At the time, I thought the Certified Public Accountant that we had was good, but in hindsight I was wrong; they did our tax return for us, but after learning accounting from a college course standpoint, I realized that there are a number of things that they did not show us. The first accountant was a glorified tax preparer that basically did our taxes but didn't teach us anything in the accounting space that would have given us insight on better managing our cash flows or managing our operations. It's vital to get an advisor that gives you directions on things you should do with your income, advises you on how to grow your income, and teaches you some best practices in finance management. You want your CPA to be knowledgeable and be willing to share with you how to support your business in terms of processes, whether you are a cash or an accrual type of business. We did both cash and invoiced types of business transactions, but our function was on a cash basis, and we really needed to be on an accrual basis and understand what accrual accounting process meant.

Understanding financial statements from the standpoint of knowing the purpose of your P&L, Balance Sheet, and Cash Flow statements purpose was and is very important so that you know how to make buying decisions, how to make operational changes, and how to take cash into your business and use it in a fashion that benefits you or even to make a decision to use cash because sometimes what's in your bank account is not necessarily what you are able to spend. Having accounting knowledge and understanding is crucial to understanding your business's financial wellbeing. Understanding the management accounting process and having a CPA that advocates strictly for small business is vital in every stage of business development.

Our last CPA firm was a great company, but we were not cohesive enough as a group to follow their recommendations. They provided candid and straightforward advice, yet we were complaining amongst ourselves and had no real bonds, which in turn prevented us from understanding our roles and the conditions of our operations.

What We Missed: Takeaway - Certified Public Accountant

Get your team on one accord so that you can heed advisors' advice. When engaging our last CPA, I realized that my family and I were poorly aligned. Take courses in accounting so that you can understand the accounting process for external and internal needs. Part of the missing elements of the relationship with our first CPA, was our lack of understanding accounting, so he may have given us what he felt we could understand.

The need for a **business attorney** for us was very difficult to fulfill, primarily because the cost to hire an attorney was outside the budget of our small business, along with many today. The city in which we ran our businesses did not have attorneys with business backgrounds, that we were aware of.

The desire not to reach out to counsel outside your area for help, or wanting to stay within a ethnic group, can limit your access to counselors with a breadth of knowledge in the business arena.

What We Missed: Takeaway - Legal Counsel

Dealing with legal counsel for all our business existence was a hit-or-miss process. We found a limited number of legal counselors that were forthright in giving advice and guidance. My tips on getting good legal business counselor is doing your homework, unless you have come across one from a positive experience.

Seek references from other business associates and peers, check out the background with the local bar associations, and do some research. Recently, I Googled an attorney that was recommended by a new business acquaintance and found out that he was being reprimanded for handling a client's relationship poorly.

We didn't have resources like Google in our time, and one of the advantages of cyberspace is the increased access to information. When interviewing attorneys, create a list of what your needs are, and ask about their background in dealing with the concerns of your business, by requesting examples from client cases they have resolved.

Today, the legal climate has changed. There are many specialists in all aspects of business law, who help with startups, estate planning, real estate, contract law, and many others.

Setting up a legal fund when you start would be a great idea; a pre-emptive strategy to guard against unforeseen incidents.

Knowing that legal fees can be very expensive, there are some resources out there that can help you. Using services like www.rocketlawyers.com, the Tax & Legal Play Book by Mark J. Kohler, CPA and Attorney, and other online services will benefit business owners in terms of guidance, documentation, and getting information that is crucial to helping your business grow. And take classes on business law

Our **insurance agent** is another scenario where it's key to learn business best practices when you don't have someone around you to guide you and say, "use this guy and not that guy," or compare pricing.

Our insurance agent was a customer, so we were loyal because he was doing business with us. A bit naïve at best, we did business with this gentleman for many years only to find out that we were overcharged premiums, so we probably covered many of his Mercedes-Benz payments. After purchasing our new equipment for our commercial laundry, we were advised to get a quote from another agent and found that we could reduce our premiums by over $1,500 per month. This was quite shocking, though not abnormal with small business owners. We had a resource with the National Federation of Independent Businesses, but never sort a quote from their insurance affiliates. One of the reasons for staying with our agent was our interest in promoting a business professional from our community. What we learned from this experience is that you must keep everyone honest; if they can take advantage of you, they will.

What We Missed: Takeaway - Insurance

The advice that I would share with anyone on business insurance or any insurance, is to get new quotes every year. Two or three new quotes will give you useful information to see what the market rates are. Get references from other business owners on what they have so that you can better understand the kind of coverage you might need. Look at all aspects of your business needs. Make it broad; don't just look at the basic business coverage.

This should be a mission depending on the type of industry and size of your business, which will be a critical part of your insurance requirements. Key man (or Directors & Officers) insurance will become vital as your company grows, ensuring that the owners and senior managers in your organization is a very important part of risk management for your business longevity. A review of your policies coverage of your equipment, errors and omissions should have careful consideration. Does your policy coverage include disaster occurrences if your business encounters a natural catastrophe or storm; it can help with revenue coming into your operation while rebuilding or during extended power shortages?

So, carefully study your insurance plans, I know it takes time to do this, but read the fine print and ask many questions about your insurance agent. A good agent or independent agent should be able to shop to get you good quotes from their best carriers. Additionally, do an evaluation of your business from a risk management perspective so that you can address items that may cause you to pay higher premiums.

In working with **consultants,** the irony of my experience is that I had dealt with a very high-level consultant in my real estate and business finance experiences, with Bob Dewey who was a consultant in the projects we were engaged.

What I learned from hindsight is that I responded like most businesses I deal with today when approached by a consultant; the fees stunned me. Coming from a consultant mindset, many years later I realized the mistakes I made when a former head of personnel approached us about the consulting for our business, and the rate that she offered blew my mind. It wasn't an exorbitant rate, but I had never dealt with hiring a consultant, so it's something that I ran from as opposed to engaged. I could have used this lady's knowledge and the resources that she offered. She was offering help in the administrative side of our business, which was something that we sorely needed, and she probably could have helped us resolve a lot of issues before they were created, like help with hiring line staff and the general manager. Her $150 per hour was a nominal fee in relation to the problem she could have helped us to solve. The management skills that were brought to the table were of a greater benefit than the upfront dollar amount. Back then, we were like so many small business owners I engage with today, who cannot see the intangible benefits.

What I Missed: Takeaway - Not Hiring a Consultant

1. Turning away the consultant's offer to help in our business was being fearful of what was offered, and not knowing how valuable the offering was.
2. If you get an offer from a good consultant, do your due diligence to determine if they are worth what they are offering. If so, hire them if you are having

problems managing your business, employees, finances, technology; struggling with building your brand, or experiencing many other issues that influence your success. Hire a consultant that has the expertise in your area of need, one that has your best interest at heart, and listen to their advice.

3. Look at it not just from the affordability of what you can do right now, but look at it from what it can bring you on a near-term and longer-term basis.

4. Can they provide you with results that make sense? Nevertheless, they must answer these questions:

5. What are their deliverables? What are they going to solve for you?

6. Do they have experience in the key areas you need to be addressed?

You want to make a list of things that you need help solving and share that with your consultant so that they get a better understanding of what's going on in your operations.

Transparency will be the greatest benefit to you; they cannot help solve your problems if they do not know what problems exist.

Advisory issues with many small businesses is often a result of not having or not taking advantage of key advisors. I understand the fear one can have in terms of hiring these advisors, but it would be my advice to look for and use your network of friends and associates and other business contacts to find good advisors. Don't give up on the idea of good advisors. They are the first people that you reach out to when business problems arise, which is an ongoing process. You need them; they are beneficial to your business, and they make the difference whether you stay in business.

Create an Advisory Board: This was always a vision that I held for our company but was never able to accomplish. I had several prospects that I wanted to organize an advisory board, but was never able to get to a level of initiating the process.

Select three to five seasoned business owners, professionals, and community leaders that you trust, who can help you with your business issues, operational needs, business growth, and finances. The group should meet once monthly, but you must be brutally transparent, so select carefully who these advisors might be. Someone that you've had a chance to observe their personality, skills, and interactions with others. This will be a volunteer role until the business can afford annual board fees.

What I Missed: Advisor Takeaways

1. Trying to manage and guide your business without these talented advisors is practically an impossible feat. Select wisely be patient on your selection and you may have to go through several to find the best fit.

2. Transparency is a must, if you are not honest with your advisors who can you trust. If they have the wisdom and experience they will prevent you from making life changing mistakes.

3. A good networking group can provide you with a source of great advisors. Do your homework by checking out the background of any perspective professional, check reviews, references unless they come from a most reliable source.

4. A Board of Advisors can be very beneficial to your company; however, you must make it beneficial to the potential members. They will more than likely be very busy, so make engagement and meeting as flexible as possible. Preferably, members that have either industry knowledge, respected in your business's community, someone with high morale's and integrity.

"As iron sharpens iron, so one man sharpens another."

Proverbs 27:17 (NIV).

Conclusion

The purpose of this writing is to encourage people not to be afraid to look at the negative thing in life as opportunities. If you have limitations, problems, disasters, complications, or complaints, always face them. The worst thing you can do is to ignore them or do nothing. With the right perspective, all of these conditions are opportunities; yes, it's hard, it does seem impossible, but only if you chose to think that overcoming is impossible.

As business owners, make it a purpose if you need to hire help, find a way to pay a good wage, and look for the best possible staff. It may be hard; however, if you are looking for long-term stability, excellent staff members add great value, and helps you to grow income and stability. Don't take shortcuts in employing the right person(s).

One of my greatest weaknesses was looking at my mom through rose-colored glasses; I think for a long time I refused to see that she didn't have the skills needed to manage the business adequately. I also presumed that the limited experience I had attained in the real estate field had prepared me with administrative skills required to manage a business.

What is clear today from my now many years of experience is that you don't necessarily need all these skills yourself, but you do need to know how to find the right parties to join your team and manage them effectively. You do need to recognize your weaknesses and take corrective action. Don't miss opportunities by thinking you must do everything by yourself. If you want growth, you must be willing to allow others to be on your team.

If you have found yourself where we were many years ago, first don't feel alone as I did for so many years, there are many resources available. If you have not found a way that can help to address your problems, the answers today are often just a search engine click away. Don't follow another of my many mistakes, after being advised by a director of a state government agency to start using the internet in 1992-1993, but did not heed his advice.

Other *what I missed,* just as what many millions of young and old persons have missed while growing up in life of not being connected in my history and family, which can often lead to a life of missed opportunities and lack of focus.

I wrote this book for personal healing reasons, as well as healing for many millions of young and older persons who have not forgiven or found a clear way to basic life skills from living a life of missed relations, in their family life, which later manifest in missed opportunities in their work, business, home, and social life. How growing up in an unhealthy family really affects your life, but it does not control the outcome of your life.

How did I overcome? By finally realizing that change first must happen in me. Finding a way to develop myself, and stop looking for answers in others, particularly those without a positive change mindset.

It took many years after creating 5 different operations in our family businesses before I learned that *what I missed* the most, was a solid family developmental foundation which is what I wanted in the first place, more specifically a relationship with my mom, who would not tell me who my dad was. What is profound about our situation was that she didn't know how to create relationships with me or my siblings.

What I have come to grips after trying over and over to reach a point of peace and being ok with myself as I am right now, is to forgive. Once I reached that realization of being OK (at peace) in myself, then I recognized how much I was missing by dwelling on my missing parental relationships, I found peace with myself, I began to self-actualize, as Abraham Maslow would state it.

Missed socialization skills often are a result of our early childhood experiences; we copy the habits, actions, and views of the adults we grow up with, whether positive or negative. Make it a purpose to improve your socialization and leadership skills, by attending leadership programs that specialize in leadership socialization and leadership coaching and training.

Make learning a way of life; this is where you will find many of the answers to your problems. Hold a view of being prepared and belief that your problems exist for you to solve them.

If you gained help from this printing, post a comment on my website. If you are struggling with business problems that have you overwhelmed schedule a free 30-minute consultation to see if our service can help or apply some of the tips listed in each chapter takeaways.

You can gain great insight by reviewing information in this book, upcoming workbooks, workshops, subscribe to our email newsletter and updates on our website www.equinnconsulting.com.

*There is no passion in playing small – in settling for a life
that is less than one you are capable of living.*

Nelson Mandela

You are more than a human being, you are a human becoming.

Og Mandingo.

Goals are dreams with deadlines.

Diana Scharf Hunt

The vision must be followed by the venture. It is not enough to stare up the stairs- we must step up the stairs.

Vance Havner

Do not let your past circumstances, family, community and thoughts, control your present, which is your gift for change. What you are thinking and doing right now can transform your life. It's your choice what your tomorrows will be, good, bad or indifferent!!!

Bill Quinn